Original title:
Tree of Life Tales

Copyright © 2025 Creative Arts Management OÜ
All rights reserved.

Author: Gideon Shaw
ISBN HARDBACK: 978-1-80566-786-5
ISBN PAPERBACK: 978-1-80566-806-0

The Forest's Embrace

In the forest where laughter roams,
Squirrels dance and find their homes.
A wise old owl tells silly jokes,
While plants play cards with playful blokes.

Raccoons in hats spin tales of glee,
Chasing shadows by the old oak tree.
Frogs croak tunes that make us chuckle,
As the breeze whispers with a soft snuggle.

A Symphony of Saplings

Young sprouts gather with joyful shouts,
Practicing tunes of wiggles and bouts.
Mice hum along, tapping their toes,
While butterflies flutter with stylish bows.

A banjo toad joins in the fun,
Under the rays of the warming sun.
Each tiny leaf sways with delight,
In this giggly concert, everything's right.

Vines of Connection

Vines entwine in a goofy dance,
Twisting and twirling, they take a chance.
Bumblebees buzz with a playful grin,
As flowers blush, where laughter begins.

The sun peeks down, tickling the leaves,
While chipmunks plot as the mischief weaves.
Laughter grows high, like branches of fun,
In this playful world, we all are one.

Harvesting the Horizon

The orchard's ripe, with fruit so sweet,
Yet squirrels sneak off with sneaky feet.
They giggle and munch, in a comical craze,
Planning their feast for silly old days.

In the fields, crops share their dreams,
Whispering secrets in giggling streams.
With each harvest, a chuckle's born,
In this bountiful place, joy's never shorn.

Silhouette of Seasons

In winter's coat, the branches freeze,
Squirrels dance, as if to tease.
Spring begins with blooms so bold,
While leaves gossip tales of old.

Summer's sun brings shadows wide,
Creatures frolic, no need to hide.
Autumn shows off colors bright,
Pumpkin hats in playful sight.

Whirlwind of Wildlife

A raccoon laughed, with tiny paws,
Stealing snacks without a pause.
Birds chirped in a feathery choir,
While ants plotted their grand empire.

The fox winks, with sly delight,
As bunnies hop, what a silly sight.
Turtles slow dance, beating time,
With rhythms sweet, it feels like rhyme.

The Language of Leaves

Whispering secrets on the breeze,
Leaves debate, with such great ease.
Some shade tacos, some shade pies,
A salad serves as leafy spies.

In autumn, a crunch, a cheer!
They laugh as they tumble, without fear.
Winter's bare stage, a silent drift,
But spring brings tales, a lively gift.

Sapling Songs

Little saplings sing off-key,
Stretching upwards, bold and free.
With twigs as arms, they dance and sway,
In playful games, they find their way.

Each tiny leaf joins in the fun,
Casting shadows, giggles run.
Grow up quick, but take your time,
Every moment's a silly rhyme.

The Branching Pathways

In the forest where squirrels meet,
A raccoon danced on little feet.
He slipped on leaves, oh what a sight,
His friends all laughed, it was pure delight.

Beneath the branches, shadows play,
A crow tells jokes in a funny way.
With cackles loud, he claims his fame,
But his puns? Oh, they're pretty lame!

Stories Beneath the Bark

Knots in wood, they spin a tale,
Of a snail who dreamt to sail.
With a leaf as a boat, and a rain drop map,
He slid and slid, then fell with a flap.

A wise old owl rolls his eyes,
At silly critters and their lies.
"Not all who wander are lost," he hoots,
But some just trip on their own roots!

Echoes of Ancient Roots

Deep in the ground, they gossip and chatter,
The roots share secrets, oh what a matter!
"Did you hear about the bug that can dance?
He spins and twirls, it's pure happenstance!"

The elderly bark, with wrinkles so wise,
Cracks jokes like it's the best surprise.
They chuckle softly in the soft night,
As the stars join in, twinkling bright.

The Green Heartbeat

Leaves rustle softly, a gentle cheer,
As grass tickles toes, drawing near.
A caterpillar boasts, not a single qualm,
"I'll be a butterfly, just wait for my charm!"

Beneath a bright sun, beetles groove,
In their shiny suits, they make a move.
The world is a dance floor, oh so sweet,
In this lively place, life's a funny beat!

Beyond the Trunks

In a forest where squirrels wear hats,
The branches gossip like old house cats.
Leaves fall like confetti when they throw a bash,
Dancing with acorns, oh what a clash!

The owls tell jokes late at night,
While raccoons perform in the soft moonlight.
A pup and a breeze race through the foliage,
Squeaks of laughter fill every cottage.

But beware of the wise, grumpy old crow,
Who claims he knows everything, just so you know.
He squawks about wisdom like it's a prize,
While the other birds roll their eyes and sighs.

Beneath the trunks, life's a grand affair,
Filled with odd creatures who just don't care.
So gather 'round, let the stories unfold,
In a place where the silly hearts are bold!

The Story Weaving Roots

Deep in the ground, where secrets are spun,
Roots share gossip and have lots of fun.
They giggle about the bugs with their quirks,
And host grand parties beneath the smirking firks.

The daisies tell tales of sunshine so bright,
While mushrooms provide snacks for the night.
The ladybugs dance in their polka-dot dress,
Making the underground a total success.

A wise old tortoise narrates with flair,
Of the garden's drama and all its despair.
While critters lean in, with ears perked up high,
They burst into laughter 'til they're dry as a pie.

As roots weave their stories, the world comes alive,
From silly shenanigans, new tales will derive.
So laugh with the leaves, and wiggle your toes,
In a place where imagination blissfully grows!

Songs of the Silvan Soul

In a grove where the willows twirl and spin,
The wind sings a tune of joyful din.
Chirpy little creatures join in the play,
Making musical mischief throughout the day.

The crickets compose a melodious beat,
While the rabbits keep rhythm, oh so sweet.
A frog leaps high, making everyone laugh,
As he croaks a solo on a leafy staff.

The sun dips low with a twinkling grin,
Painting the sky like a violin.
Fireflies twinkle, a lighthearted glow,
Guiding the revelry to and fro.

In this whimsical land, no frowns are found,
Where notes are exchanged with joy all around.
So play on, sing out, let the fun take its toll,
For laughter and music bring life to the soul!

Chronicles from the Orchard

In an orchard where apples wear glasses and hats,
The fruit holds meetings and chats with their spats.
Cider-making contests spark laughter all day,
As pears twist their stems and giggle away.

The branches gossip about the last rain,
While bees paint the blooms with sweet, sticky grain.
A butterfly DJ spins tunes from his groove,
As critters all gather to dance and to move.

But beware of that sneaky old worm on a spree,
Who claims he's the answer to 'What's under the tree?'
He wriggles and winks, causing quite the debate,
While the whole orchard laughs, saying, "You're late!"

So munch on some fruit and join in the cheer,
Where funny and sweet make the best atmosphere.
Chronicles abound where the silly unfold,
In an orchard of laughter, bright and bold!

Emblems of Endurance

In the garden, a broccoli stands tall,
Waving at veggies, it's having a ball.
Carrots gossip, and peas start to dance,
While cucumbers dream of a summer romance.

An old oak chuckles, its branches so wide,
He tells the young saplings, 'Just enjoy the ride!'
A squirrel in a tie joins the humor parade,
As acorns throw parties that never do fade.

Bees buzzing loudly with stories to share,
Of flowers they flirted with, unaware.
The tulips all gossip, with petals so bright,
While daisies just giggle, 'Oh what a sight!'

Amidst all the laughter, sunbeams play hide,
In this leafy world, we're all bonafide.
From veggies to flowers, there's joy to ignite,
As nature's own circus puts up a delight!

Harmony of Habitat

In the forest, the critters hold court,
A raccoon reads tales with a trash can report.
An owl rolls his eyes at the gossiping crow,
While deer just giggle, enjoying the show.

A choir of frogs sings a croaky tune,
As the fireflies waltz to the light of the moon.
The flowers all sway, in a fragrant ballet,
While a squirrel rehearses for the part of the day.

Red pandas munch bamboo, making no fuss,
'You think your diet's tough? Try eating like us!'
Bees buzz with jokes, 'Pollinate or die!'
As laughter erupts in the blink of an eye.

This habitat dances, with rhythm and cheer,
Together they thrive, the message is clear.
In the heart of the woods, where we feel divine,
Nature's a party, it's one of a kind!

Roots and Wings

With roots digging deep, and wings so wide,
The birds laugh at grasses that try to reside.
'You can't fly like us, perched high on your thrones!'
'But we hold the ground, we're kings of our stones!'

A snail in a shell dreams of soaring through skies,
While crickets compose tunes, aiming for highs.
The flowers chime in, feeling so bright,
As they twirl to the rhythm of day into night.

A wise old tortoise shuffles around,
'Who needs to fly when you own the ground?'
With laughter and glee, each creature declares,
In this dance of the life, there's joy in their lairs.

From butterflies fluttering to bugs on a spree,
Every friend has its charm, wouldn't you agree?
Roots hold us steady, while wings set us free,
Together we thrive, like coffee and tea!

Whispers of the Canopy

In the canopy high, where the parrot does chat,
The monkeys swing by, 'Did you hear that?'
Leaves rustle secrets, a soft leafy cheer,
While a wise old tree winks, lending an ear.

A chameleon blends in, with colors so bright,
'I've changed my look twice just to see the light!'
The sloths hang around, taking their precious time,
While squirrels hold contests in acorn-climbing prime.

In this layered kingdom, each critter adds flair,
From the drumming woodpecker to the butterfly pair.
They gather to giggle beneath the sun's beams,
Sharing funny tales woven from whimsical dreams.

As evening approaches, the stars start to shine,
A glow-worm recites poems, making all feel fine.
In the whispers of leaves, laughter shimmers bright,
In this lively haven, everything feels right!

Echoes through the Undergrowth

In the shade, a squirrel hops,
Chasing dreams and acorn pops.
Leaves chatter with a giggly breeze,
While ants march on, doing as they please.

A toad sings a tune, quite off-key,
Hoping to woo a passing bee.
The mushrooms dance in polka-dot caps,
In this wild, wacky world, no one naps!

A rabbit tells jokes to a sly old fox,
Who laughs so hard, he loses his socks.
The hedgehog snorts with mirthful glee,
As nature's stage holds a comedy spree.

Together they share a hearty laugh,
Crafting delight from Nature's art.
In the wild whispers, joy is found,
Echoes of laughter wrap around.

The Language of Lichen

On cool rocks, lichens have chats,
Their greenish tones wearing funny hats.
They laugh at moss, who feels quite gray,
Saying, "We take colors in a brighter way!"

With a wiggle, they spread and grow,
Forming shapes like a funny show.
A snail joins in, with a slow-motion dance,
While the lichen giggles, giving him a chance.

"Why did the tree blush?" one lichen jokes,
"I saw the bark bare—now that's no hoax!"
The others chuckle, their voices light,
As they paint the rocks, a scenic sight.

Whispered secrets in the damp and cool,
Lichens teach us, old nature's school.
In hues of green and wrinkled cheer,
They speak of life, both far and near.

Branching Out in Time

An oak tree grins with ancient glee,
Telling tales of long ago, you see.
"I saw a squirrel in a fedora hat,
He thought he was cool, imagine that!"

With branches stretching, reaching high,
The branches wave like arms in the sky.
"Let's do the twist!" the limbs all shout,
Dancing wildly, pulling leaves about.

Each ring tells time, a story bold,
Of seasons growing, both hot and cold.
The wind joins in, a twisty dance,
While the roots giggle, catching a chance.

Through ages past, and moments bright,
Nature's humor fills the night.
In every crack, in every line,
Lies laughter, timeless and divine.

Tales Softly Whispered

In the hush of night, the shadows play,
As critters tell jokes in their own way.
A fox yips loud at a badger's jest,
While the owl hoots, claiming he's the best.

"Why did the crow sit on a telephone wire?"
"Because he wanted to be a little higher!"
The fireflies blink, offering bright grins,
In this nightly gathering, all are wins.

Squirrels crack up over pinecone pies,
As raccoons steal snacks, with mischievous eyes.
A hedgehog rolls in tosses of bark,
While the trees prepare for a larking spark.

Whispers of laughter float through the night,
Nature's comedy, a pure delight.
In every rustle and gentle sway,
Tales softly whispered lead the way.

Life's Intertwined Branches

In the garden of laughter, we all sprout,
Twisting and turning, there's never a doubt.
The branches get tangled, but that's just the game,
We all share the sunshine, we're never the same.

Silly squirrels dart with acrobatic flair,
While birds tell their secrets without a care.
Roots stretch like dancers, they wobble and bend,
Each knot brings a giggle, a riotous friend.

The leaves whisper stories of mischief and fun,
As shadows play tag when the day is done.
We play hide and seek with the rays of the sun,
In our branchy abode, we're never outdone.

So raise up a toast to this whimsical crew,
Growing together, it's all we can do.
With laughter and joy, our spirits align,
In this tangled up chaos, oh isn't it fine?

Flourishing in Silent Growth

Under the surface, things wiggle and jive,
Roots throw wild parties, feeling so alive.
You'd never know chaos rises below,
While branches above put on quite the show.

With each little twist, a new tale to tell,
As critters make homes where the wild stories dwell.
A cactus with laughter, a flower with sass,
Blooming so brightly, they all have a class.

The sun beams a joke that the shadows all tell,
While the wind hums a tune from its magical shell.
In stillness and silence, the giggles abound,
Amongst leafy whispers, where fun can be found.

So next time you ponder the quiet of green,
Remember the party that's joyfully unseen.
Flourishing together, though hidden from view,
Our laughter grows wildly, a riotous crew.

The Cycle of the Seasons

Winter's a joker, in frostbitten glee,
He throws snowball fights, oh can't you see?
With mittens and laughter, we bundle up tight,
As icicles giggle in cold winter's light.

Spring bursts with cheer, she's a bubbly delight,
Colors are splashed, everything feels just right.
She dances with blooms and twirls in the rain,
Sprinkling bright giggles, no sign of a stain.

Summer's the charmer, with sunshine galore,
He's grilling and chilling, and then he'll encore.
Picnics and games, with lemonade sweet,
Tickling bare feet on warm, sandy heat.

Then autumn arrives with a funny old song,
He prances in leaves, where the colors belong.
Snap, crackle, pop, all the crunch in the air,
Seasons roll round, with a whimsical flair.

Whispers of the Wilderness

In the wild where the critters gossip and chat,
A squirrel named Ned is the boldest of that.
He tells all the tales of the nuts that he steals,
While waving his tail, oh what a big deal!

An owl in spectacles, wise and quite spry,
Reads stories of mischief to stars in the sky.
He hoots with a chuckle, delivering glee,
As fireflies gather, a luminous spree.

The fox shares their secrets with giggles so sly,
While rabbits hop in, with laughs oh so spry.
Every rustle and flutter holds laughter quite well,
In whispers of nature, where stories dwell.

So take a wise moment to listen and learn,
The wilderness beckons, it's time for your turn.
With every soft whisper, in shadows and light,
The joyous tales blossom, oh what a delight!

Mirth Beneath Maple

In a shady grove, squirrels chat,
Telling tall tales, goofy and fat.
They argue who's fastest on furry feet,
While ants dance around to a funny beat.

Leaves shake and giggle with every breeze,
A wobbly raccoon climbs, trying to tease.
He slips and he slides, a hilarious sight,
As laughter ignites in the warm sunlight.

A wise old owl hoots with glee,
Challenging critters to climb the big tree.
The prize is a nut—golden and bright,
In this merry realm, everyone's light.

So come gather 'round, join in the fun,
As goofy goings-on are just begun.
Under hues of green, let your spirit soar,
With giggles and chuckles, who could ask for more?

Flora's Fables

A butterfly painted in colors so bold,
Tells a tale of a worm, once covered in mold.
He rolled into a ball, claiming his fame,
And danced when he turned into fluttering flame.

A beetle with glasses amusingly said,
"Life gets brighter when you keep your head!"
With whispers of grass and chuckles of flowers,
They share wild stories of nature's hours.

The daisies giggle when clouds roll in,
As raindrops fall down, it's a splashy win!
Slipping and sliding, they laugh all the way,
In a carnival world where all dare to play.

So pranksters of petals, do spread the cheer,
In Flora's domain, let out your dear laugh here.
Let stories and smiles bloom all around,
As every small critter creates the sound.

The Gift of Gnarled Limbs

With branches twisted in delightful knots,
Gnarled limbs sing songs of fanciful plots.
A raccoon named Fred, quite the prankster, you see,
Swaps hats with a turtle, oh what a spree!

Under this canopy of whimsical cheer,
The woodland creatures all gather near.
A squirrel juggles acorns, a sight quite absurd,
While crickets play tunes, their legs all a-burred.

Come gather beneath this quirky old bark,
Where shadows are plenty and mischief can spark.
Birds crack wise jokes, laughter fills the air,
In this playful haven, there's joy everywhere.

So swing by the branches, take part in delight,
In a world where the silly is always in sight.
With gnarled limbs offering warmth and fun,
Join the joyous ruckus, everyone! Run!

Heroines of the Hardwood

In a forest lush, where heroes abide,
Stand sturdy young maidens, with nature as guide.
They wield sticks like swords, charming and spry,
With a giggle and wink as they aim for the sky.

The squirrels and rabbits all cheer with delight,
As the heroines battle the shadows of night.
With courage like thunder and laughter like rain,
They dance amidst foliage, bringing no pain.

One swings from a vine, but oh what a mess,
Landing in leaves in a flowery dress.
The chorus of laughter erupts from the trees,
As comrades unite in the soft summer breeze.

So here in the glen, where adventure is rife,
Join the heroines' tales—such is sweet life!
For every small giggle and every loud cheer,
Brings the magic of friendship, ever so dear.

Chronicles of the Greenway

In a forest, where giggles grow,
The squirrels wear hats, don't you know?
Raccoons dance under the moon's soft glow,
While owls play poker, stealing the show.

A rabbit tells tales of a carrot race,
With vegetables cheering from their place.
The beetles tap dance with such grace,
While the trees sway with a smile on their face.

The sun shares jokes with the playful breeze,
As butterflies flit with the utmost ease.
A frog croaks rhymes with such expertise,
It's a comedy club for the forest's keys.

So gather 'round for a playful tale,
Of woodland friends who never go stale.
With laughter and joy, they set the sail,
In the land where humor will always prevail.

The Age of Acorns

In a kingdom of acorns, small and bold,
Where stories of laughter are often told.
The mighty oaks, with leaves of gold,
Hold secrets and chuckles from times of old.

A chipmunk juggles with shiny nuts,
While the wise old owl gives clever cuts.
He says, 'Life's best served with laughs and guts,'
As the acorns roll and the humor struts.

A squirrel's got jokes; he's quite the hit,
Sharing punchlines that perfectly fit.
While the bunnies hop, they never quit,
Finding humor in each little bit.

So toast to the acorns, round and fun,
For their laughter-filled stories have just begun.
In this playful age, all woes are undone,
As each giggle echoes in warm forest sun.

Seeds of Stories

Tiny seeds whisper tales of cheer,
Of mischief and laughter year after year.
With roots intertwined, they gather near,
In a patch where the sun brings warmth, no fear.

The daisies gossip with colorful flair,
About a gopher who lost all his hair.
While the daisies serve tea in a comfy chair,
The chopped-up grass laughs; life's never unfair.

A sunflower spins tales of trips gone wrong,
Where bees buzzed off with a curious song.
The seedlings laugh, saying, 'Come along!'
In a garden where silliness makes all belong.

So sow these seeds, with whimsy and glee,
For stories sprout in much brighter spree.
In this patch of joy, you'll always see,
That laughter and love are the real decree.

History Held in Hollows

In the hollows of trees, where stories dwell,
Echoes of laughter begin to swell.
A badger named Bob spins tales quite well,
Of famous mischief in the forest shell.

A raccoon recounts a grand heist night,
Where snacks went missing, such a delight!
The woodland critters had quite a fright,
As whispers of giggles took joyous flight.

The mice write songs about blunders and spills,
While crickets chirp with evening thrills.
In the shadows, friendship fulfills,
Creating a world where laughter instills.

So come and listen, don't be shy,
For the hollows hold joy that will never die.
In the heart of the trees, come give it a try,
With history's humor reaching for the sky.

Shadows Beneath the Leaves

In the park where all things grow,
Squirrels plan a nutty show.
They wear tiny hats with flair,
Plotting dances in the air.

Rabbits join the leafy dance,
Wiggling tails as they prance.
A worm named Fred tries hard to sing,
His voice is squeaky, like a spring.

Echoes of the Earth

Beneath the roots, the whispers flow,
A hedgehog tells a joke, you know.
The frogs all laugh, they leap in glee,
While ants declare, 'We've got a spree!'

An owl peeks with a wise old grin,
Says, 'Why did the sprout want to win?'
'Cause growing tall was quite the scene,
He'd reach the sky and eat ice cream!'

Fragments of Flora

A daisy turns to gossip grass,
'You won't believe who drank the sass!'
The tulips giggle, rolling tight,
As petals dance into the night.

A thistle whispers, sharp and keen,
'Bet I can steal the garden queen!'
But bees just buzz with sleepy heads,
Too busy dreaming of sweet breads.

Celestial Saplings

Little sprouts reach for the stars,
With tiny leaves like fancy cars.
They argue whose shade is the best,
While cracking jokes, they never rest.

The moonbeams tickle every stem,
As ladybugs form a cool gem.
Underneath the starlit sky,
They giggle, wink, and wave goodbye.

Buds of Hope

In the garden where dreams sprout,
Buds of laughter twist about.
Some bloom fast, while others wait,
Each one thinking, "I am great!"

Squirrels chatter, dance around,
While butterflies drift unbound.
The sun winks, a playful tease,
"Go on, sprout, do as you please!"

Raindrops giggle on the leaves,
Telling tales of silly thieves.
They stole sunshine, what a laugh,
Now the flowers are the staff!

And when the breeze decides to play,
Buds of hope bloom bright today.
They giggle, twirl, and wave in glee,
In this garden, wild and free!

The Body of the Earth

The ground's a tummy, soft and round,
Belly laughter in the sound.
Worms and bugs play hide-and-seek,
In this soil, nature's peak!

Mountains are the body's grin,
Valleys curve like knees within.
Rivers flow like a cheerful sigh,
Nature's giggles passing by.

Clouds are pillows, fluffy and bright,
Whispering secrets of pure delight.
The sun's the heart that beats each day,
Giving warmth in its own way.

From roots to skies, they join the spree,
A funny dance, so wild and free.
The earth chuckles with a sway,
In its own quirky, charming way!

Connecting Through the Bark

Woodpeckers knock on the sturdy door,
"Hey! Anyone home?" they'll implore.
Branches wave, a greeting shout,
Connecting friends, there's no doubt!

Squirrels gossip, tails in a twist,
Sharing secrets, they can't resist.
"Oh, did you see that funny crow?
He tried to play with a river flow!"

Lizards lounge, basking in glee,
While ants march on, so busy and free.
They high five the bark with a shimmy,
Nature's dance, all oh-so-quirky!

So let us clap for this merry crew,
Beneath the canopy, green and blue.
Laughing together, what a spark,
In this world where friends leave their mark!

Petals of Experience

Petals flutter with snickers and glee,
Each holds a tale, just wait and see.
Once there was a rose who'd boast,
"I'm the brightest!" She'd smile and toast.

Then came a daisy, funny and spry,
"Compared to you, I'm a butterfly!"
They laughed, adorned in their floral wear,
Sharing bites of sunshine and fresh air.

A tulip chimed in, feisty and proud,
"I dance in the wind, I'm bright and loud!"
Nature's ensemble, humorous and grand,
Each petal a story, unplanned.

So gather round, from far and wide,
To hear these tales, with petals as guides.
With giggles and chuckles, they fill the sky,
Experiences bloom, oh my, oh my!

Seasons of Serenity

In spring, the blossoms dance with glee,
The bee's bum wiggles, oh so free!
Squirrels argue over acorn stash,
While flowers bloom in a colorful splash.

Summer sun brings a picnic feast,
Ants march in lines, a culinary beast!
A lazy cat naps on a sunny branch,
While frogs croak out their water dance.

Autumn leaves start to twirl and twirl,
A squirrel in shades, oh what a whirl!
Pumpkin spice makes everyone cheer,
As children laugh with Halloween near.

Winter's chill, a snowman's cap,
Bunnies hop in a fluffy trap!
Hot cocoa's served with a big marshmallow,
As we watch the snowflakes flurry and flow.

Stories Woven in Green

In a forest bright where laughter's found,
A fox dressed up in a tutu spun round.
Rabbits gossip about carrot delights,
While owls hoot under starry nights.

Bees tell tales of the flower's sweet,
While ants parade in synchronized beat.
Chipmunks juggle nuts with a wink,
Oh, nature's show packs quite a blink!

Each leaf a page in timeless lore,
With whispers of breezes forevermore.
Squirrels giggle at their own tall tales,
As branches sway and the laughter sails.

Amidst the green, the tricks unfold,
Of critters bold and stories told.
Nature's stage, the quirks and plots,
From sunny days to the chilly spots.

Canopy of Dreams

Under the boughs where dreams take flight,
A raccoon sings into the night.
With stars as his backup band on high,
While fireflies glow like a flashlight sky.

Parrots squawk with colorful flair,
While monkeys swing without a care.
The canopy whispers playful schemes,
As creatures chase their wildest dreams.

A bear attempts a dance so grand,
But trips on roots, it's not what he planned.
The forest giggles, a chuckling crowd,
As the bear blushes, not too proud!

And when the sun gives a sleepy wear,
The dreams get cozy, floating in air.
The laughter lingers, a gentle stream,
In the heart of the woods, we all can dream.

The Arbor's Memoir

Once I sprouted, oh what a sight,
With joyful winds, I danced with delight.
A little sapling with big aspirations,
Nature's laughter, my true foundation.

Birds nested high in my flowing hair,
Each morning's song, a sweet affair.
Squirrels joked about whose spot was best,
While I stood tall and gave them rest.

Seasons changed, I shed my coat,
Leaves swirling down like a colorful boat.
Children climbed to play hide and seek,
Their giggles filled me for the whole week!

Now I'm older, with wisdom to share,
A gnarled trunk, yes, but still full of flair.
With roots so deep, I tell tales anew,
Of laughter and joy, and the sky so blue.

Branches of Existence

In a forest where squirrels plan,
The acorns plot to take over man.
Twirling branches, they do dance,
While leaves giggle at their chance.

Raccoons argue, who's the best?
The winner claims the softest nest.
With laughter ringing through the skies,
Even old owls can't hide their sighs.

Bouncing bunnies join the fun,
Making mischief in the sun.
They hop and skip, they're full of cheer,
While deer just roll their eyes and steer.

As twilight comes, they start to chat,
About the weird things that they spat.
In this realm of joy and jest,
Each creature knows they're truly blessed.

Whispers in the Canopy

In the branches, secrets float,
A chattering parrot starts to gloat.
"Did you hear what the crow did?"
"Spread it fast, don't let it skid!"

The woodpecker drums a tune,
Attracting squirrels out by noon.
Frogs start croaking in delight,
Under the stars, they hop in flight.

The owls hoot, sending a tease,
"Who's falling asleep among the trees?"
The wind picks up their chuckling song,
As night descends, all join along.

With playful banter and silly tales,
Through rustling leaves, the laughter sails.
A canopy of whispers bright,
In this world, all hearts take flight.

Roots of Wisdom

Beneath the ground, the roots conspire,
To share tales of past—what a fire!
"Did you hear about the lost shoe?"
"Not just one, I've found a few!"

They whisper stories to the earth,
Of every critter, joy, and birth.
Old worms wiggle with delight,
"Let's gossip till the morning light!"

A spider spins with such finesse,
Crafting webs of sheer impress.
"Catch a breeze? Or maybe flies?
Let's have a contest; let's win the prize!"

Beneath the smiles, with wisdom shared,
In every root, a story bared.
Laughter echoes through the soil,
In every tale, the world's a foil.

The Living Tapestry

In the woods, a fabric grows,
Stitched with laughter, care, and woes.
Each thread a creature, bold and bright,
Woven stories in pure delight.

The badger knits a cozy cloak,
While rabbits tease with hop and joke.
The hedgehog thinks it's quite a mess,
"You'd better tighten those, I guess!"

A parade of ants march in line,
Carrying crumbs like they're divine.
The grasshoppers laugh, do a jig,
As the butterfly shows off her gig.

With twinkling stars above their heads,
They dance and spin on leafy beds.
In a tapestry of fun and cheer,
Every creature holds laughter dear.

The Legacy of the Land

In the heart of the soil, worms wiggle and squirm,
Telling tales of the past, with each juicy turn.
Now, the mole's on a quest, his nose in a knot,
Searching for treasure, or just a hot spot!

The grass whispers secrets, its blades all ajive,
With each passing breeze, they wiggle and thrive.
The daisies gossip about the bees' dance,
While the old oak just snores, missing all the romance!

The sunbeams play tag, while shadows just hide,
As squirrels crack jokes, taking life in their stride.
Even the ants have a party at noon,
Dancing around crumbs, under the bright moon!

With laughter and joy, the land sings its song,
A delightful mishmash, a party so strong.
From roots to the sky, the legends unfold,
In this crazy old world, there's magic untold!

Flux of the Forest

In a forest so wild, the leaves do a dance,
With squirrels on stilts, putting on a prance.
The rabbits wear hats, and the birds sing along,
While the brook splashes joy, its bubbly, bright song.

The mushrooms are giggling, sprouting with flair,
Hey, watch out for bears, they're unaware!
The fox in his mischief, sets traps with a grin,
Hope the deer don't notice their game about to begin!

The pine trees whisper, "What's the latest scoop?"
With critters in clusters, it's a wild troop!
The snails bring the wisdom, slow as a breeze,
While the raccoons just shrug, munching leaves with ease.

From dawn till dusk, this mischief unfolds,
In a whirlwind of laughter, as each story is told.
Nature's grand comedy, it twists and it bends,
A circus of life, where chaos transcends!

Rich Rhythms of the Roots

The roots stretch and curl, in a lively ballet,
Twirling in silence, as night turns to day.
They gossip with rocks, "Did you hear what they said?"
A worm interrupts, "I just found some bread!"

The beetles roll dice, as roots tap out beats,
While shadowy moles dance, with their wiggly feet.
Even the soil hums, in a symphonic trance,
Creating sweet music, for the critters to dance!

With laughter and chatter, the underlife thrives,
In this playful planet, where fun always dives.
Sunlight spills laughter, through the canopy high,
As the roots keep the rhythm, beneath the blue sky!

Oh, to be a root, feeling all the spright,
Joining in mischief, till the fall of night.
With giggles and grins, they weave chapters of cheer,
In this whimsical world, where joy perseveres!

The Wisdom of Willows

Beneath the wise willow, the kids come to play,
With branches like arms, they never sway.
They tell old stories of rabbits so bold,
While the breeze adds a twist, making them gold.

The wise one just chuckles, its leaves start to sway,
"Hold tight to your dreams, let them lead the way!"
The frogs on the banks croak a magical tune,
As the night sky rolls in, wearing a bright moon.

With giggles and whispers, wise secrets abound,
As the roots underground share tales that astound.
In the shadowy glen, laughter is found,
While the wise willow smiles, keeping joy all around!

So sit by the willow, let your worries take flight,
In the giggling woods, everything feels right.
Embrace all the laughter, let your spirit align,
For the wisdom of willows is truly divine!

Guardians of the Grove

In the grove where critters play,
Squirrels dance the day away.
Owl wears glasses, thinks he's wise,
But can't find his way to the skies.

Rabbits race with feet so quick,
Frogs perform their best cool trick.
Bees gossip about their hive,
While ants march on a pastry drive.

A tortoise plays chess with the breeze,
And whispers secrets to the trees.
With acorn hats they do parade,
Each one hoping to get laid!

In the shade, a sloth orders snacks,
While raccoons plot against the packs.
With giggles loud and laughter bright,
The guardians keep the grove in sight.

Chronicles of the Canopy

Up above where branches weave,
The laddered ants can't believe.
A parrot tells a tall, dumb tale,
While owls roll eyes, drinking ale.

The sunbeam dances, flicks a bee,
Who stings the cat up in a tree.
The frog jumps high just for a thrill,
But slips and falls with quite a spill!

The tree frogs croak a song off-key,
While butterflies sip their herbal tea.
A chameleon plays peek-a-boo,
His colors change – that sneaky view!

From squirrel to crow, they all find cheer,
In this chronicled canopy full of beer.
With laughter echoing, day turns night,
In tales where even bark can bite!

Cacophony of Colors

Leaves of gold and shades of red,
A parrot sings from its cozy bed.
The colors clash, a joyful sight,
As chipmunks giggle in delight.

Berries burst with flavors grand,
While frolics happen across the land.
A skunk gives flowers quite a fright,
And runs away like a comical flight.

A raccoon juggles shiny things,
While the jokes fly on feathered wings.
Crickets chirp in rhythm strange,
In this wild world, nothing's out of range!

Rainbows arch through skies of blue,
With laughter twinkling as the dew,
It's a colorful riot, full of cheer,
Where even a worm can disappear!

Treetop Reverie

In tree branches where dreams take flight,
A dreamer snores, a curious sight.
With leaves for pillows and stars for light,
In this treetop, all feels just right.

Squirrels debate the best acorn brand,
While raccoons steal the birds' last stand.
A wise old crow in shades of grey,
Tales of folly show us the way.

A sloth hangs low, still as a log,
While dancing daisies tease the fog.
With whispers of wind and giggles galore,
The treetops echo, "Come, explore!"

On moonlit nights, the owls will croon,
A magpie argues with the moon.
In this dreamy space, all shadows play,
As leaves twirl down, throwing caution away!

The Wisdom in the Wood

In the forest, wise old roots,
Whisper secrets, wear bright boots.
Squirrels gossip, branches sway,
Chipmunks dance, come join the play.

Beneath the bark, a riddle sings,
Fungi giggle, sprout their wings.
Trees chuckle, their rings proclaim,
Life's a jest, it's just a game.

Once a bird schooled a brown hare,
"Fly with flair, give life a care!"
But the hare tripped, fell on its rear,
Crows cawed loudly, shared the cheer.

Roots entwined, a funny sight,
Bouncing bugs, what pure delight!
Laughter echoes through the wood,
Nature's humor, oh so good!

Mysterious Mossy Memories

Mossy pillows, tales to tell,
Covered critters, all is well.
A slug recited Shakespeare's verse,
While a snail sold dreams—oh, curse!

Beneath the cloak of emerald fluff,
Mice hold parties, never enough.
"Who's your cousin?" one mouse would ask,
"Let's raise a toast, that's quite the task!"

One day a raccoon found a hat,
Danced with joy, how about that!
Said the owl, "Now that's a sight,
Start a style, give fashion fright!"

Memories weave through mossy trails,
Tickling notes on nature's scales.
Every mushroom holds a joke,
In the forest, laughter's bespoke!

Under the Bow of Time

Under the arch, time sways slow,
Beneath the leaves, laughter will grow.
A turtle claimed, "I'm fast, just wait!"
While a rabbit smirked, "You're really late!"

In the shade, a wise frog croaks,
"Life's a joke, or so it pokes."
Bees hum tunes, the sun shines bright,
Dancing flowers, oh what a sight!

A shadow plays with each heartbeat,
With every giggle, we find our feet.
Under the bow, time spins its tale,
Where every whimsy sets the sail.

Laughter gathers, like a breeze,
Bouncing branches, rustling trees.
In this space, we share our rhyme,
Living free, under the bow of time!

The Unfolding Canopy

High above, the leaves are bright,
Whispering jokes, oh what a sight!
A monkey swings with flair and zest,
While a parrot tends to his nest.

Among the branches, antics thrive,
Creatures laughing, they come alive.
A gopher claimed, "I'm quite the chef!"
But served acorns—everyone left!

Branches dance, a wobbly show,
While a crow sings a silly low.
"Why did the worm cross the path?"
"To find its friend and share a laugh!"

Underneath the branches' weave,
Joyful moments, we believe.
The unfolding tales of canopy,
Show life's silliness, wild and free!

Sprouts of Tomorrow

In a garden where laughter blooms,
Little sprouts weave silly costumes.
With leaves of green and roots so bright,
They dance till the stars wink goodnight.

Chasing butterflies, they twist and twirl,
Whispering secrets to each little curl.
Ants march by in a comical rout,
While the worms join in with a squiggly shout.

Sunshine tickles with rays so warm,
Giggling buds causing quite the swarm.
Each petal opens with a wide grin,
Who knew that plants could be such a win?

Giggles grow tall, reaching for the sky,
As bees buzz along, happily spry.
Tomorrow's sprouts, with stories to share,
Will conquer the garden, flair beyond compare.

Echoes of the Woodland

In the woodland, echoes play,
Squirrels chatter throughout the day.
Birds gossip about a lost shoe,
While raccoons plot their next big coup.

The owl hoots with a wink so sly,
A tree stump laughs as squirrels fly by.
Mushrooms giggle in their cozy nooks,
While rabbits sing tales from their storybooks.

A brook babbles jokes, flowing with cheer,
Making frogs croak loud for all to hear.
Under the ferns, a snail does a dance,
While beetles applaud with a clumsy prance.

The laughter in woods, a grand symphony,
Each creature plays their role so free.
Together they create a woodland spree,
Where every echo tells of glee.

Leaves of Legacy

Leaves of legacy flutter and sway,
Sharing old jokes from back in the day.
They whisper secrets of ages past,
About how the time has scooted so fast.

Old branches chuckle, with bark worn thin,
As stories of squirrels playfully spin.
A wise old leaf offers sage advice,
"Don't take life too seriously, it's nice!"

The roots underground tap dance to the beat,
While bugs in the bark compete in the heat.
Each grain of soil holds tales untold,
Making every moment a sight to behold.

So let's attend this joyous parade,
Where laughter and wisdom will never fade.
To honor the leaves, a grand celebration,
Of giggles and sprout-rooted inspiration!

Beneath the Ancient Boughs

Beneath the boughs that stretch so wide,
Silly shadows frolic side by side.
The grass tickles toes with playful delight,
While critters plot mischief 'til night.

The ancient trunk grumbles with pride,
As squirrels take the wildest ride.
Rabbits hop with hats a'la mode,
Chasing the breeze down a secret road.

A family of ants plays peek-a-boo,
While a lazy lizard starts dreaming too.
The sun shares jokes with a downy plume,
While roots beneath rumble in playful gloom.

So gather 'round for tales of fun,
Beneath the boughs where laughter's begun.
In this magical realm, joy meets the land,
With giggles and grins, together we stand.

Folklore from the Forest Floor

Once a squirrel stole a shoe,
Wore it proudly, who knew?
He danced on logs, oh what a sight,
Chased by crows in a goofy flight.

A wise old owl thought he could sing,
But all he did was squawk and fling.
The rabbits laughed, the foxes too,
'We preferred your hoot, who knew?'

Under mushrooms, secrets lurked,
Frogs held court and giggled, smirked.
A turtle raced, oh the thrill,
But fell asleep, uphill, what a chill!

In shadows where the shadows play,
Laughter echoes, night turns to day.
Ghostly giggles fill the air,
Nature's jokes, everywhere to share.

The Soundtrack of the Seasons

Spring sings sweet, with blooms aglow,
Bees buzz by, putting on a show.
The breeze hums songs of sunny delight,
While ants tap dance, oh what a sight!

Summer tugs with warmth and cheer,
Crickets chirp, oh so near.
Beneath a sun, there's quite the parade,
A snail in shades, how it's made!

Autumn's here with a rustling tune,
Leaves crunch underfoot, it's a boon.
A pumpkin laughed, its belly shook,
"Guess who's the star in my spooky book?"

Winter whispers with chilly fun,
Snowflakes waltz, oh what a run!
A bear in pajamas, and sleds all around,
In this frosty land, joy can be found.

Looming Legends in Leaf

A pine tree claimed it had magic power,
Said it could rain down candy every hour.
But all it dropped was pinecones and grit,
"Sweet," said the critters, "but not quite it!"

An old oak bragged with limbs spread wide,
"I'm the tallest, I won't hide!"
But when the winds blew with a mighty sound,
It swayed so much, it nearly fell down!

A budding vine thought it could rhyme,
"Vines are cool, we take our time!"
But tangled up in such a flub,
It tripped a fox—it was a club!

Legends whisper in the leaves and breeze,
With every giggle comes a tease.
For in this woodland, tales are spry,
And laughter floats beneath the sky.

Grace Within the Grove

In the grove, where laughter flows,
A rabbit prances, showing off its nose.
With each hop, it spins a yarn,
Telling tales of flowers that charm.

A hedgehog twirled beneath the moon,
Promising to sing a little tune.
But instead, he snored and snoozed,
While the crickets looked quite confused.

Mice held parties inside a husk,
Dancing wildly, full of brusk.
They'd nibble cheese and giggle in glee,
"Just wait till dawn, you'll see, you'll see!"

Grace in the grove, oh what a sight,
Where critters gather, day and night.
With stories spun like webs of fun,
Join the laughter, everyone!

Leaves of Memory

In a park with ghosts of past,
A squirrel stole my sandwich fast.
I chased him up a giant oak,
He laughed and said, "Just a joke!"

Each leaf fell like a twist of fate,
My picnic now a food debate.
The trees whispered with a grin,
"Next time, bring nuts, you might win!"

While reminiscing by the stream,
Insects buzzing, quite the dream.
I waved to all the bees on spree,
They buzzed back, "We're busy, see?"

So here I sit, my meal all gone,
In this leafy realm, getting drawn.
With laughter ringing in the air,
I'll come again, without a care!

Fragments of the Forest

In a thicket, branches bend,
A chipmunk spots me as a friend.
He cracks a joke about his stash,
Says, "Stealing nuts is quite the flash!"

The flowers giggle in delight,
Telling secrets through the night.
A tale of vines that wrap too tight,
And vines responding, "It's alright!"

The mushrooms dance, a funky crowd,
All beneath the branches loud.
A rabbit hops, declares with glee,
"I'm the king of hide and seek, you see!"

Through whispers of the winds so free,
Nature chuckles, zestfully.
In this forest, wild and bright,
Even shadows find delight!

Nature's Endless Narrative

A bear was reading 'Hunger Games',
While otters played their silly games.
The logs all rolled their painted eyes,
As deer recited their alibis!

The clouds above pretended to snore,
While birds performed on forest floors.
A parrot squawked a pirate tale,
Infected laughter, windswept gale.

The flowers wore their brightest hats,
With butterflies as diplomats.
They talked of peace in pollen trade,
And how good vibes just can't fade.

As laughter rings from tree to tree,
Nature's narrative spins carefree.
With every rustle, every shout,
Life finds ways to laugh it out!

Shadows of the Old Growth

In the twilight, shadows loom,
Old trees whisper tales of gloom.
Yet squirrel chortles from the ground,
"Why so serious? Look around!"

The owls hoot their nightly jokes,
While raccoons plot with sneaky pokes.
The shadows dance, they twist and twirl,
Each story shared makes laughter swirl.

Amidst the trunks that wear some scars,
Crickets chirp like little stars.
"A shadow can't catch a bright spark,
So join the fun, don't miss your mark!"

And so it goes, the night unfolds,
With laughter told by the trees so bold.
In old growth's heart, where tales unite,
Every shadow finds its light!

Gnarled Legends

In a forest where the whispers dwell,
An old oak tells jokes, and sings quite well.
Squirrels gather, all ears to the ground,
For punchlines hidden where acorns are found.

A bearded birch boasts of storms it has faced,
Dancing in winds, never outpaced.
With bark like a crown, it reigns like a king,
Making the shyest of critters all sing.

The wise willow chuckles while swaying its limbs,
Reciting old fables, but the punchline swims.
"Why did the seed break up with the soil?"
"Too clingy, my friend, it found that quite toil!"

And as twilight falls, shadows begin,
The tales of the trees always end with a grin.
Nature's comedians, they tickle the mind,
In this leafy cabaret, laughter you'll find.

Nature's Timeless Narratives

The pine tree tells tales of pinecone parades,
Of squirrels in costumes, in nature's charades.
Under the stars and the moon's gentle glow,
They dance and they twirl, putting on quite a show.

The birches gossip of their neighbors nearby,
"Did you hear? That elm is certainly shy!
But last week it danced with a bee on a whim,
The beetles have tidings, let's share it with him!"

In the heart of the grove, a comedy stand,
The mushrooms take turns, no need for a band.
With spores like confetti, they crack silly jokes,
Leaving all critters rolling in hoaxes.

Frogs join the fun, singing tunes with the breeze,
While crickets provide beats, a symphony tease.
In every leaf rustle, there's laughter and cheer,
In Nature's grand theater, joy's always near.

The Heartwood Chronicles

In a grove where the branches stretch out like arms,
Every thick trunk has some quirky charms.
The oak claims it dated a beauty called vine,
But lost her affection for a less-ingrown pine.

The cherry tree blushes in spring's sunny light,
Sharing stories of blossoms in a colorful flight.
"I once had a dream of a fruit-based career,
But I rolled with the punches and now I just cheer!"

A giggling sapling, just starting to grow,
Dependencies shifting, leaves all aglow.
It claims that it learned from a wise old lime,
To take life with laughter, no matter the time.

And when dusk descends, with a glimmer of jest,
The night wraps its arms 'round their leafy fest.
Under a blanket of stars shining bright,
The Heartwood debaters are in for a night.

Blooming Through Ages

Petals chuckle in colors so bold,
Each bloom shares a secret, a memory told.
The violets tease roses for being so red,
"Who needs all that fuss? We're cool in our bed!"

A daisy bursts forth with a whimsical cheer,
"What's in a name? You can call me dear!"
While tulips stand up in elegant rows,
"Let's show the world how our beauty really glows!"

The sunflowers nod, with their heads held up high,
"Let's party together, and wave to the sky!
We brighten the days, just watch our big smiles,
While hiding our seeds in the ground for a while!"

And as twilight whispers to close this grand show,
Nature laughs softly, in its vibrant tableau.
For every bloom tells a joke, takes its chance,
In the garden of giggles, they sway and they dance.

Narratives in the Neotropics

In a jungle so thick, a sloth had a dream,
To dance with a monkey, oh how it would beam!
But the sloth was so slow, he tripped on his toes,
And the monkey just laughed, saying, "Look at him go!"

Then the parrot, quite wise, had a tale to share,
About the nutty squirrel with a wild, fluffy hair.
"He stole all my snacks!" the poor chipmunk cried,
While the squirrel just grinned, on his treasure he pried.

A toucan announced, with a honk and a squawk,
"Who needs a watch? I just go by the clock!"
But time flew away, as he sat on a branch,
Dreaming of fruit and a jungle-wide dance.

In the end, they all laughed in this home of delight,
Where stories of mischief made every day bright.
With each twist and turn, in this vibrant domain,
Adventures keep flowing like the sweet, gentle rain.

Echoes of the Evergreen

Among the tall pines, a frog found a lute,
In search of a band, he began to hoot!
With a turtle on drums, they rocked to the beat,
While the crickets joined in, what a quirky feat!

A hedgehog with glasses gave advice too wise,
"Don't wear your spines, dear! You'll give folks a surprise!"
But the hedgehog just grinned, in style he believed,
Said, "Fashion's a party! You should be relieved!"

As the sun dipped low, an owl caught a wink,
"Why do trees stand tall? To keep secrets, I think!"
With a wink and a nod, he hooted with glee,
While the squirrels held acorns like cups of sweet tea.

In this woodland choir, all creatures unite,
Tales told in the whispers, under moon's shining light.
Each chuckle and cheer a reminder to see,
The laughter in nature, forever carefree!

Breath of the Forest

A lizard named Larry liked to strut with flair,
In shades of green, he'd dash here and there.
But one day he slipped—oh, what a blunder!
He landed right smack on a pile of thunder!

An ant with a parachute took off from a hill,
He soared through the air—what a daredevil thrill!
But his landing was messy, with a tumble and roll,
While a snail cheered him on, saying, "You've got soul!"

Then the wise old raccoon offered snacks and a plan,
"Let's host a feast, with all critters we can!"
So a party ensued with a dance and a cheer,
Where everyone's laughter made the forest appear.

In the breeze there was joy as they wiggled and spun,
Each creature in harmony, oh what fun had begun!
With the breath of the forest, so lively and light,
They danced till the dawn, in the glow of the night.

Stories Sprouted in Soil

In a patch of brown dirt, a gnome brewed his stew,
With mushrooms and roots, oh, what a fine view!
But a worm wiggled close, saying, "Hey, what's the fuss?"
"I'm hungry for tales, come share or you'll rust!"

Nearby sat a cat with a hat, quite absurd,
Who claimed he could talk to each flying bird.
While the sparrows discussed, with laughter so bright,
The cat scratched his chin and said, "Isn't life light?"

At dusk, all the critters found joy and delight,
As stories of old spun a wonderful night.
From the largest of trees to the tiniest bug,
Each tale brought them close, like a warm, cozy hug.

So they laughed and they played, from the soil to the sky,
In their little kingdom, friendships would fly.
With each silly story that blossomed and grew,
The spirit of soil brought them together, it's true!

Roots of Resilience

In the garden of giggles, roots go deep,
They whisper of woes, where the flowers creep.
With nimble twists, they dance in disguise,
Even when storms brew, they just crack jokes and rise.

A wiggly worm said, "I'm the best wrangler!"
The grass just chuckled, "You're a weird dangler!"
Through floods and droughts, they poke out their heads,
Sharing silly tales with their leafy friends.

Under the ground, where the sproutlings joke,
A mushroom chimed in, "I'm the king of the poke!"
With fungi humor and roots that can tease,
They giggle through seasons, just doing as they please.

So if you feel heavy, unroot your frown,
Join the plants in laughter, let joy come around.
With roots in the soil, let your spirit fly,
In this quirky universe, life's a fun nigh!

The Harmony of Hidden Life

Beneath the bright canopies, things roam and sway,
A squirrel named Chuck had a house party today.
He served acorns in cups, with a mushroom dip,
While critters did the cha-cha and the hedgehog flip.

The ants set a conga line, moving in sync,
While the snails took their time, they needed a drink.
They laughed at the sun, so hot on their backs,
Sipping dew drops and taking sweet naps.

Crickets played symphonies, frogs croaked along,
Creating a beat that felt really strong.
The world turns wild when the sun starts to fade,
Hidden life hums a tune; in shadows they wade.

So join the good giggle, let the leaves tell your tale,
In forests of folly, let your spirit set sail.
For in every whisper, in every old tree,
Lies laughter and joy, just waiting to be free.

The Green Pages of Existence

In the library of greens, what wisdom we find,
Little sprouts tell stories, they're not far behind.
With every leaf flip, there's laughter and cheer,
Read on, if you dare, but don't shed a tear!

The wise old oak says, "I've seen lots of things,
From squirrels in tuxedos to birds wearing blings!"
While ferns flip their pages, "Oh, look at the jest!
Who knew life's a book, and we're all at the fest?"

Through seasons of giggles, the tales have their quirks,
Like mushrooms in tuxes and dancing old jerks.
They spin funny yarns of the forest's great schemes,
Where laughter grows freely, and joy's sewn in dreams.

So open up wide; soak in nature's delight,
Every page brings a new joke and a light.
In this green bound volume, with stories to share,
Life is all laughter; it's our merry affair!

Traces of the Timbered Past

Once there stood a tree with tales to unfold,
It whispered to the breeze, "Oh, what have I told?"
With knots full of wisdom and limbs wide with smiles,
It shared all its secrets, through the sunbeam styles.

From bark to the branches, all danced in the breeze,
Tiny bugs with capes engaged in sweet tease.
A beetle named Fred wore a hat made of pine,
Claiming it was vintage; how snazzy, how fine!

The leaves would gossip, rustling loud and fast,
They snickered at memories of the timbered past.
With each little shiver, a chuckle would flow,
These were the echoes of laughter below.

Though logs may grow old and the seasons may change,
The humor remains in this woodland exchange.
So treasure the stories, let laughter outlast,
For life's a grand punchline, tied to the past.

Swaying into Tomorrow

In the breeze I dance and sway,
Leaves tickle me, come what may.
Squirrels race, a nutty chase,
While I wiggle in this place.

Bumblebees buzz, what a sound!
Flower friends all around.
A frog jumps high, oh what a sight,
I chuckle softly with delight.

The sun peeks through my leafy lace,
I hear whispers from the space.
A chipmunk's joke brings me to tears,
I sway and giggle through the years.

As dusk arrives, the shadows play,
I practice my best dance today.
Tomorrow comes, I'll sway some more,
What funny tales from branch to floor.

Fragments of Foliage

Once a leaf, now a story untold,
Drifting down, I'm getting old.
I met a bug who wore a hat,
He claimed he's royalty, imagine that!

Dancing with acorns in the sun,
Silly tales of laughter and fun.
I overheard a branch's joke,
It tickled me until I broke!

A gust of wind sent me amiss,
I twirled through air, oh what bliss!
Chasing clouds, I found a crew:
The giggling leaves and morning dew.

In the autumn, colors clash bright,
Turning trees into a sight.
Fragments of laughter fill the day,
As we flutter and dance our way.

Sunbeams and Shadows

Under sunbeams, shadows play,
I wiggle while the critters sway.
A rabbit hops, it seems so light,
Disco moves in the sunlight!

The crow caws out a silly tune,
While a snail joins, oh how he zooms!
A squirrel in shades, so cool and sly,
Wonders if he can touch the sky.

Butterflies flutter, in chaos they swirl,
Trying to impress, oh what a whirl!
I laugh and sway in this joyous weather,
With sunbeams and shadows, we're all together.

When the moon peeks, stars light the way,
In the dark, we continue to play.
Whispering secrets from night to dawn,
Our funny adventures just carry on.

The Shelter of Seasons

Springtime sprouts, the buds pop free,
Little critters dance with glee.
A ladybug twirls, feels so grand,
While I sway in the soft, warm sand.

Summer's heat brings sun and fun,
Picnics shared and races run.
A chipmunk juggles while I cheer,
With laughter echoing ear to ear.

Autumn whispers, the leaves turn gold,
I tell stories that never get old.
A crow plays tricks, oh what a sight,
Scaring squirrels, gives me delight.

Winter wraps us in blankets white,
Snowball fights in the moonlight.
Seasons change, but what remains,
Are funny tales that break the chains.

www.ingramcontent.com/pod-product-compliance
Ingram Content Group UK Ltd.
Pitfield, Milton Keynes, MK11 3LW, UK
UKHW021528210125
4208UKWH00025B/513

9 781805 668060